A PRIMER:
the art of
NATIVE AMERICAN BEADWORK

with projects

Z. Susanne Aikman

Cover Design: Z. Susanne Aikman
Text Design: Z. Susanne Aikman

FIRST PRINTING MAY 1980
SECOND PRINTING APRIL 1981
THIRD PRINTING AUGUST 1982
(Revised & Enlarged)
FOURTH PRINTING MAY 1986
FIFTH PRINTING JUNE 1987
SIXTH PRINTING AUGUST 1988
SEVENTH PRINTING MARCH 1989
EIGHTH PRINTING NOVEMBER 1989
NINTH PRINTING JUNE 1990
(Redesigned)
TENTH PRINTING APRIL 1991
ELEVENTH PRINTING APRIL 1992

Printed in Dallas, Texas U.S.A.

Video & Book available from:

RΘ♂ DⱠꟻꝰꙮꙄ

MORNING FLOWER PRESS
P.O. BOX 11443
Denver, Colorado 80211

ISBN 0-9629155-0-5

*Beadwork design greeting cards and inspirational jour-
nals are available at your bead shop or write us for
information. They are unique and beautiful.*

WADO *Morning Flower*

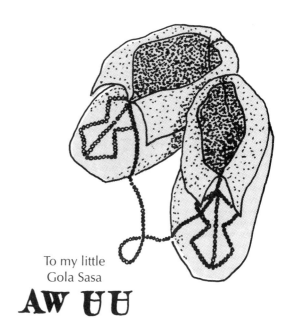

To my little
Gola Sasa
AW ƱƱ

CONTENTS

Thanks to everyone who answered questions, proofread, and did all the little things that helped bring this project together. Special thanks to my students, past and future, for asking questions.

FOREWORD

This collection of instructions was first put together for my beadwork class at Denver Free University in 1979.

Over the past 20 years I have practiced the beadwork craft and learned techniques from other artisans of many tribes and areas.

My influences are from books, museums, private collections, fine artists and the creation at large. I want anyone interested in this unique American Indian style as well as a fashion industry craft to learn the basics and practice the techniques so that beadwork as an artform will not become static or lost in our fast-changing world.

May the knowledge within this book bring much honor to your lodge. You have brought honor to mine by desiring to know these things.

Wado. **GV**

INTRODUCTION

Glass beads were first introduced to the western hemisphere by the Columbus expedition in 1492.

Bead trade began in North America in the 1700's. The seed bead was introduced in the mid-1800's from Venice, Italy. About 1885, a finer bead from Czechoslovakia was traded and most surviving work is done with Czech beads.

Early colors fluctuated with area, trader, and availability. Backgrounds were usually white or light blue, probably because these were more available and red being most prized because of its rarity.

The meanings of designs were and are inherent to the worker. Although there are designs and/or colors characteristic to certain areas or tribes, still the individual design meaning if any, was and is distinctive to the artist.

There are many types and styles of beadwork introduced herein, but by no means is this or any other reference material all inclusive or a final word in this area.

Use your imagination, bring your life experiences to your work and create unique and personal designs by combining these various instructions. Consider producing exclusive contemporary pieces with lasting value and quality as well as exceptional traditional items.

Start a scrap book or use the note pages in this volume to keep ideas, articles, pictures, drawings, etc. for your beadwork. It may be a reference collected today won't inspire a project for months, but all resources are very useful at some time – keep them.

Visit museums, shows, trading posts, galleries, pow-wows, any place beadwork or designs might be shown.

Inspect the work closely and learn from other artisans. Ask questions – respectfully and intelligently. Most craftpersons will gladly share information with you and maybe you will learn something from each other.

One important belief you should learn and use is the Spirit bead. Each piece should contain an intentional mistake or Spirit bead. The reason for this is that we are but human and cannot achieve perfection; if we attempt perfection in a piece it could be bad luck. So always remember your Spirit bead.

Challenges will be encountered at every turn when you begin. Be assured you are not the first to encounter these problems nor will you be the last. We all have and do cope with frustrations in our beadwork, but creativity, logic and experience will help you overcome.

Some common problems you will find are:
- Threading fine beading needles
- Knots in the thread
- Beads with holes too small
- Irregular beads
- Mis-counting in your pattern
- Broken needle eyes
- And most common will be tired hands and eyes.

When you begin beadwork few tools are necessary, but there is no substitute for beginning with quality materials.

BEADS

Quality glass Czechoslovakian or Italian seed beeds make the best work. Japan is importing seed beads, but of lower quality in sizing, shape and color choice. Good beads will usually be sold on strings in hanks or kilos. Occasionally they will be loose, but be sure to find out where they were made. Small packages or vials of loose beads are generally not a good buy in seed beads or the best quality.

Seed beads come in a variety of types of beads. A very scarce type is the **_glass cut bead_** from Czechoslovakia. These are beads with flat polished sides to make light reflect and disperse giving the bead a cut gem quality and unsurpassed beauty in the work. Seems the Czechs have stopped exporting this cut bead so it is rare to find any and expensive to purchase. Japan has begun producing a bead they call "cut," but they do not come near the quality and beauty of the European cut.

Colors in seed beads are many and like dye lots in any other industry they will vary slightly from batch to batch. The opaque is the most used and common. The color is as its name implies – opaque, solid color.

The transparent seed bead is just that – a transparent glass color. With these beads your choice of thread color can influence the bead color itself, so you may want to experiment with these two variables. Also, these are very beautiful made into a hanging piece in front of a light source, similar to stained glass.

One of the most overlooked is the luster seed bead. These have a metallic-like quality and can add some sparkle to your work when you want some flash and cuts are so rare. Iris beads have soft colors with a rainbow effect, similar to the shine on a raven or polished abalone.

SIZES

I never trust a bin in the store to always be holding the bead size I am looking for. I measure a few beads in every hank I buy to be sure of the size. An approximate count per inch will save some time and money later when you are ready to use the beads.

An approximate count per inch
(averaged over 2 inches)
$9°$ = 14
$10°$ = 15-17
$11°$ = 18
$12°$ = 21-22
$13°$ = 23-24
$14°$ = 24-25
$4°$ = 45-25 Italian size
$16°$ = 27

TOOLS

NEEDLES

Needles come in many sizes and longs and shorts. Longs are best for loom work and shorts are good for sewing beads. You may find the longs are also called beading and shorts called sharps.

A Glover's Needle is a 3-sized, razor-sharp needle for sewing leather.

Generally these are the needle sizes used for bead sizes, but these sizes will vary from maker to maker so check your beads and needles for compatibility while you are in the store.

Needle Size	Bead Size
11	C° or 10°
12	10° or 11°
13	10° or 11°
14	11° or 12°
15	12° or 13°
16	13° or 16°

THREAD

Nylon filament is strong and lasting, but it stretches, frays and is stiff to work.

Polyester is strong, lasting, feels good, not too stiff and will not deteriorate. Plus it comes in hundreds of weights and colors.

Pure silk thread has all the best qualities of the other threads, as well as having a very fluid effect on fringe and glides easily though several layers of threads for repair work. Be sure knots are reinforced because the nature of silk is slippery and easily unties itself. Silk is a natural material and will deteriorate with time.

Waxed dental floss is good for warp threads and single strands when strength is important. Unwaxed dental floss is good for your teeth.

BEESWAX

A cake of pure beeswax will last you for a long time. Wax your thread to add strength and avoid knotting. If knots do occur the wax makes them easier to unknot. Cut a workable length of thread and draw it across the cake of wax. On the loom, rub the cake of wax back and forth a few times on the warp threads after you have it completely strung to save time.

PLIERS

A pair of needle nose pliers are useful in breaking uneven or damaged beads from the work.

SCISSORS

Scissors are very necessary and any good sewing shears will fill you needs.

HOUSEHOLD CEMENT

Clear household cement or nail polish is used to reinforce knots and assure their not coming undone later.

LOOMS

There are a few different types of looms ready made that you can find in your craft shop. All are practical and useful but a homemade loom is just as good and much cheaper. Mine is made of a 2x4 scrap and 4 little wood scraps, 2 small springs, a few cup hooks and some nails.

See "LOOM WORK" for details.

STORAGE

Store your beads in such a way to avoid tangles in the hanks. I use a wooden coat hanger with little nails spaced about an inch apart to maximize useable space with a minimum of storage space. Hanging in front of a window they can be enjoyed all the time.

Although hanging is a handy and beautiful way to store beads, they do accumulate dust. Wash them on the string by dunking in a mild solution of ammonia and water or window cleaner, rinse in clear water and lay flat on a towel to dry.

Loose beads can be stored in any number of available objects, including but not limited to: baby food jars, plastic deli bowls, plastic kitchenware, plastic boxes, tackle boxes, etc.

To work with the beads, I suggest small, deep saucers or coasters of light color or white. Work with a small amount of each of your design colors in one container, unless you are using colors of very nearly the same hue or value. I have found it very difficult to work from containers that are deep or have corners.

To keep from chasing your beads around a saucer, put them on a soft white cotton towel or soft fabric (like felt or short nap velvet) square, arranging the beads into a pallet formation. The beads won't run away from your needle.

STRINGING BEADS

OGLALA BUTTERFLY

1. Begin by stringing a single length of beads on heavily waxed, doubled thread or waxed dental floss to desired length for a necklace or bracelet and tie into a circle. Be sure the necklace is long enough to go over your head.

2. Use waxed single thread from here on.

3. Second row will go through every third bead, adding three new beads between.

4. Third row will go through the center bead of the second row, adding five new beads between.

5. Fourth row will go through the center bead of the third row, adding seven new beads.

The shape will ruffle and become like a delicate lace.

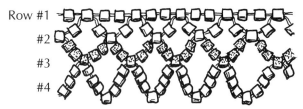

*Using the same color for rows One and Two will cause more color continuity in your piece.

Pull firmly but not too tight.

Pendant Chain Technique:
2 needle technique

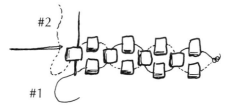

Use this chain for your pendants, rosettes, or medal-lions.

BEADED NETS

Use these stringing techniques to make collars, cover yokes, baskets or odd-shaped things. Drape lamp shades or hang in a window. Illustrations are self-explanatory and fairly easy to master.

Remember, illustrations are drawn loose; when doing the actual stitches, keep your work firm and beads close together but not so rigid that they buckle.

Horizontal Net Weave:

OR

Vertical Net Weaves:

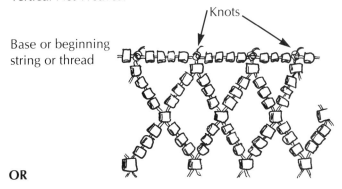

Knots

Base or beginning
string or thread

OR

Beginning Row:

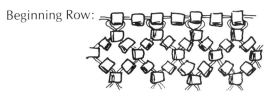

LAZY DAISY

In this design you will be working with two basic colors, a petal color and a center color of your choosing. Cut a length of thread, wax it, and thread your needle. Use a single strand for these designs.

1. Tie one petal color bead to the end of your thread.

2. String 5 petal color beads and go back through the knotted bead to form a circle of these 6 petal color beads.

Note: Imagine the beads are numbered and keep the knot tail always on the same side, long enough to hold between your fingers will be helpful.

3. Add one center color bead and go through the fourth petal color bead (toward the third petal bead).

4. Add 2 petal beads and 1 center bead. Go through the fifth petal bead in the opposite direction (toward the sixth petal bead).

3.   4. & 5.

5. Add 2 petal beads, go through the petal bead next to the new center bead and pull the beads up tight.

Repeat steps 4 and 5 over and over until you have the desired length of chain.

Finish the chain with a clasp or make it long enough to go over year head and complete the chain by connecting the last and first daisies.

EASIER DAISY CHAIN

Cut and wax a single thread.

1. Tie one petal color bead on the end of thread.

2. String 8 petal beads and go back through the knotted bead to form a circle.

3. Add one center color bead and go through petal bead #6 toward bead #7.

4. Add 2 petal beads and go back through beads #5 and #6 and again through the two new beads A & B.

5. Add 6 petal beads and go through #B only.

6. Add one center bead and repeat steps 3 and 4 until you complete a chain of desired length.

DAISIES ON A STRING

Cut a length of thread and wax it. Tie a bead on the end and single-string your chain color for about 14 beads.

1. Add 4 petal color beads and 1 center color bead (total of 5 beads).

2. Go back through the first petal bead.

3. Add 2 petal beads (#5 and #6).

4. Go back through #4 petal bead.

5. Single-string chain color, 14 beads and repeat flower.

If the flower seems too loose, add a third petal bead to the last group of petal beads.

WHAT TO DO WITH DAISY CHAINS

- Short lengths with clasp or thong sewn on the ends for bracelet or choker.

- Long lengths for necklace by itself or chain for rosette, medallion, or other fetish to wear around your neck.

- Very short lengths for earrings.

BORDERS

Borders can be used and altered numerous ways. This section will introduce variations and some uses. These are only limited by your imagination and creativity.

TWO BEAD EDGING or BLANKET STITCH

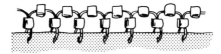

Modify this simple edging by changing the number or color combinations of beads up and/or across.

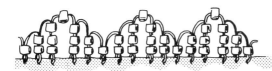 

Use tube or bugle beads
(an elongated seed bead).

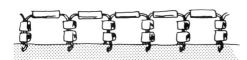 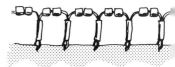

OBLIQUE EDGING

Row #2

#1

OVER CASTING

Needle goes through from back to front.

This stitch is used to cover edges of thick bases for bead-work, such as belt buckles, hair combs, barrettes, rosettes or leather pieces to finish the edge. We will discuss these items in more depth later.

I've also seen it used to decorate the edge of cowboy hats or a ball cap bill – imagine that – with cuts too. (Cut beads are described on page 3.)

Borders are used to finish loom work, rosettes, medallions, etc.

Also use them on your clothing. Border a collar, yoke seam, pocket or cuff. Dress up your jeans or plain shirt or blouse. Fancy up a lace edging or ruffle. Be sure to reinforce your knots with a drop of polish or glue and don't put your beaded garment through a wringer. With good quality thread, glass beads can be laundered without any special handling. Iron beaded garments on the wrong side with beadwork face-down on a thick towel.

BEAD FRINGE

Fringe uses are as diversified as borders. Finish a rosette, medallion, necklace, earrings, sash or ties. End the fringe with beads, shells, teeth, claws, cones, loops or quills. Once again, use your imagination.

Single Clover Shell Cone Double Loop Quill Single Loop

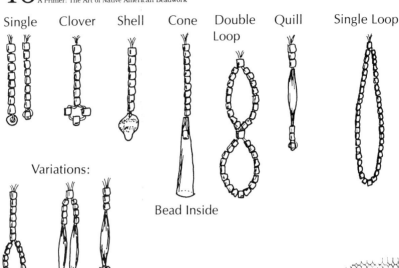

Variations:

Bead Inside

GRAPH PAPER

Work out your patterns with felt markers, crayons or colored pencils before you start. Inspiration for patterns and colors can be found in so many unexpected places. Look at wallpaper, knitting, crocheting and embroidery patterns, museum collections, blankets or rugs. See designs and color combinations in nature, old Masters' paintings, contemporary prints, computer or laser graphics. But don't overlook the expected places for inspiration: trading posts, books, and powwows.

When doing small symmetrical designs that must have a specific size (barrettes, comb or belt buckle loom work), begin your pattern in the center of the design and work out from the center on one side to on-half the desired length, then begin again at the center and work the other side to match.

Graph papers are shaded every 5 lines to help you follow your pattern across the page.

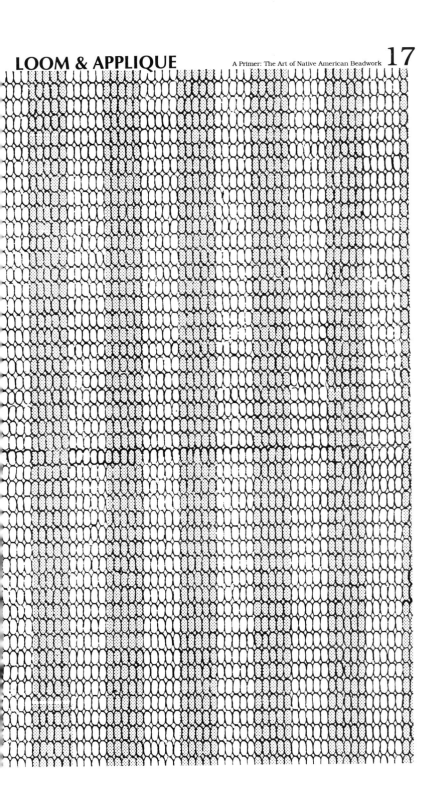

3-DROP

PEYOTE or GOURD

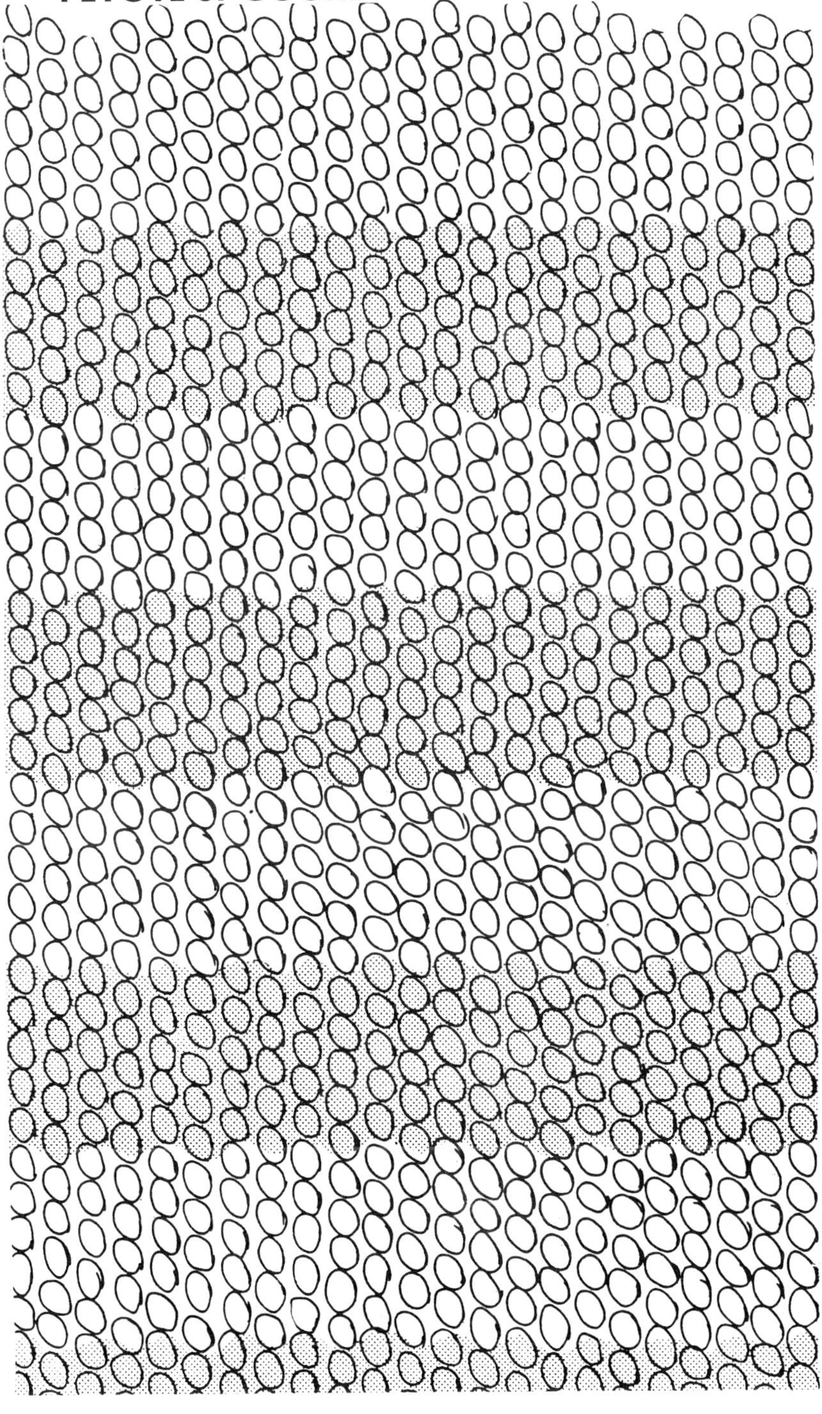

LOOM WORK

Looms vary with size of work, portability, maker, tradition, and other factors. Manufactured looms, mentioned earlier, can be purchased from most craft supply shops at reasonable prices.

Make your own loom to fit your needs. These are some I have used, seen or have directions for. You should pick the best points of each and build your loom for your needs.

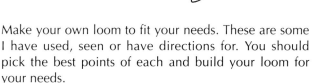

Spring

Hooks→

Ruler Marks

Moveable Piece

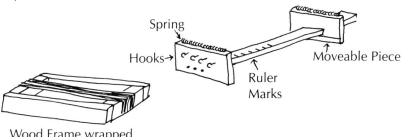

Wood Frame wrapped with Warp Threads

Small Tooth Comb

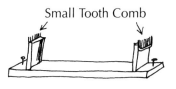

Warp Separators:

Combs

Notches

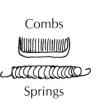

Springs

STRINGING THE LOOM

These are general instructions for use with size 11° and larger beads. Use a good quality heavy thread for your warp on most loomed pieces, exceptions being small pieces or for very small beads.

I use waxed dental floss for belts, hat or head bands, saddlestrips, shirt strips, brow bands, etc. White is generally used, but this doesn't mean you are limited to it.

String one more warp thread than your pattern is beads wide. Some double the outer warp threads for added strength.

BEGINNING

1. Thread your long (beading) needle with a workable length of thread.

2. Tie the first bead to the end of your waxed, single strand thread.

3. String the necessary remaining beads on the thread for your pattern.

OR

2. Tie the end of your thread to the outer warp thread where you intend to begin and weave several wefts of thread into the warp before beginning with the beads.

3. String the necessary combination of beads for the first row of your pattern.

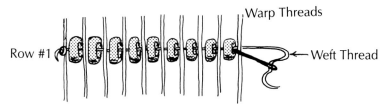

4. Place strung beads **under** warp threads.

5. With forefinger, push the beads up between the warp threads; hold them in place.

6. Pass the needle **over** the top of the warp threads, back through the beads.

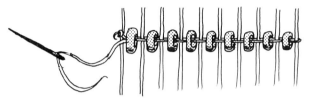

7. Pull thread tight and bring needle and thread back under the warp threads.

You are now ready to string the next row of your pattern and begin at step #4 again.

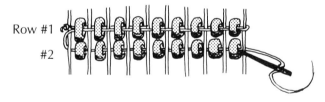

Row #1

#2

When you run out of weft thread there are a couple of ways to start a new length.

1. Pull the needle off the thread when it is too short to go on working and tie it to the outside warp thread. Be sure to tie it tight and reinforce the knot with a dot of polish or glue. Then tie the new weft thread on the other side as in the beginning.

OR

1. Before the weft thread becomes too short to work with, go back through a row to anchor the end of the thread.

2. Cut a new length of weft thread, wax it, and go back through four or five rows of beads already in place. Thus you have avoided knots altogether and reinforced the central part of your beadwork at the same time.

TO END THE WORK

After the last row is in place go back through a number of rows with the remaining weft thread. Trim all loose ends very close to the weaving, but be very careful not to cut any threads of the woven piece. Take the entire work off the loom and flatten it out on a surface.

Tie off the warp threads and tape them to the back of the piece. Use adhesive tape or an artist's tape that resists aging or glue residue that masking or cellophane tape are known to leave.

This finish is for head bands, hat bands, belts, or strips that will eventually be sewn onto something for a finish.

If you intend to use the loomed work for other creative purposes you may want to string beads on the warp threads to make a fringe or tie them in groups for a thread fringe.

PEYOTE or GOURD STITCH
(Comanche Style)

Another weaving style is the peyote or gourd stitch. This stitch does not require a loom, but does require more time as it does not work up as fast as the other styles described so far.

The basis of this stitch is like laying bricks and like bricks, are stitched on one at a time. Usually round or shaped objects are covered with this stitch, but it can be woven flat or on a base material.

Basic guide to stitch effect:

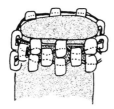

When using leather to cover a cylinder, cut the leather to exactly fit the cylinder or object and sew tightly on the object. A drop of glue under the leather will assure its staying in place on the cylinder or object.

The open cylinder (as opposed to the covered object or solid cylinder) weave is called "Crow Necklace" and is used for earrings and necklaces.

BASIC STITCH

Begin the basic stitch by stringing half as many beads as is necessary to complete one row around the object, thus leaving room to fit the next row in place, brick fashion.

The second row is started from the first bead where you started the first row. String one bead, go through next bead from first row and repeat.

OR

Begin with a single string of beads that makes one complete row on or around the base. The second row is then started by beginning at the first bead in the first row. String on one bead and go through the third bead in the first row. String one bead, go through the fifth bead in the first row. Continue to string one bead, going through the odd numbered bead until the second row is in place and pulled tight.

The next rows will now be easier, as you put on one bead you will go through the bead that is dropped down. Always end one row by going through the first bead of that row before beginning the next row.

The beads should look similar to this , the second row displacing every other bead of the first row.

Row #1
#2
#3

The gourd stitch can be done flat with some very attractive results. This is then called strip netting. But keep in mind all of these directions are for a cylinder.

WESTERN SHOSHONE VARIATION

Row #1
#2→
#3

A variation on this Comanche style is a Western Shoshone two-bead netting stitch. Simply begin as the Comanche instructions and begin the second row with 2 beads and string 2 beads instead of one.

THREE DROP or CHEYENNE

This stitch is based on a mathematical formula. The beginning number of beads on the first row must be divisible by 6 and be an even number (i.e. 30, 36, 42, 48, etc.). After arriving at the number, begin by re-moving one-third of the total beads and recount and recalculate to be sure of your figures and number of beads.

Go back through the first bead and pull thread tight, spacing beads fairly evenly around object. Add a bead and go through third bead, add a bead and go through fifth bead, and so on around. At the end, go back through the first bead on the first row. This will be the third time for this bead. Then go through the first bead of the second row.

You are now ready to begin the third row. Add a bead and go through the next "dropped" bead, add a bead, go through the next "dropped" bead and so continue the third row.

Each row thereafter is started from the first bead of the last row and a bead added between each of these dropped beads.

These directions are somewhat complicated and illustrations seem to complicate them more. I suggest you muster some patience and begin your practice piece, taking each step slowly. It is not uncommon to begin a number of times before you master this stitch.

COMANCHE WEAVE

This is a novel variation on the Peyote style, called Comanche Weave. This weave is sometimes easier to cover irregular shapes. Begin with a base material or heavy cord to start the weave.

Continue weaving and sewing beads as illustrated.

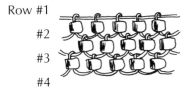

Row #1
#2
#3
#4

This weave can be left loose as shown (unlike all other directions in the book) or may be tightened for a firmer weave.

This is the basic stitch for Bugle Bead earrings found in the project section.

DESIGNS

Designs for these peyote stitches are usually a zig-zag or ric-rac type with symmetry. Flower, tipi, abstract, etc. designs are possible with this stitch, but practice is the only real way to work them out and become skilled in this challenging technique of beadwork.

ROSETTES

Rosettes are round medallions of concentric circles of beads. Either one or two needle applique technique is used with a stiff base material. Among the most useful base materials are non-woven interfacing, canvas, denim, or felt.

If your rosette is intended for use on leather the suggested practice is to produce the rosette on a separate base and then apply the finished rosette to the leather. Sewing directly into the leather for this piece would weaken the leather seriously because of the amount of stitches necessary.

1. Draw your design on the base material. You will need to know exactly where center is located and you will be sewing directly onto your drawing, so be sure it is legible and complete.

Using an embroidery hoop could be helpful for the beginner and will help you even the tension of your circles so the rosette won't buckle or pucker.

2. Sew one bead onto the base in the center.

3. Bring both needles up near that bead and string enough beads on one of the threads to fit smoothly around the center bead. This can be as few as 4 or as many as 8 beads.

4. Sew these beads to the base material with the second needle.

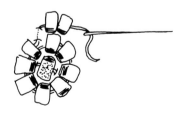

5. Continue stringing the next row and fitting the pattern and number of beads as you string.

6. Sew each row in place with second needle every three or four beads.

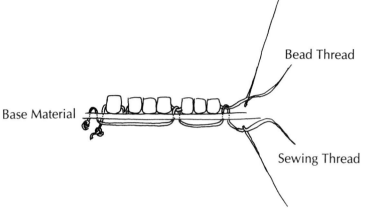

Base Material

Bead Thread

Sewing Thread

Or use this single needle approach with the back stitch. Sew the center bead in place, sew every other bead in the first circle as shown in the diagram. Then sew down every third bead from there on.

Tension is critical in a rosette. As you space the circles of beads against the previous circle, don't squeeze the new row too tight against the other beads; give them a little "breathing" room and your rosette will lay nice and smooth when you finish.

Consider starting your rosette with a button, rhinestone of concho for a new effect.

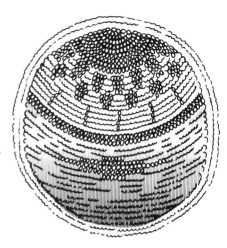

A variation of this stitch is to begin the center bead at the edge of the circle and make concentric rows over the center bead.

To fit a circle in a rectangle – as a belt buckle – complete the rosette the diameter of the shortest side of the rectangle, then continue the longer sides with concentric rows to the outer edges and finish with the overcast border.

SEWN BEADWORK

This is a stitch method to sew directly on leather or material. Real sinew was originally used and some work is still done with it today. Sinew makes very tight, solid work as it is wet while stitching.

It is usually advisable to sew the beads to a base, then apply to the garment, etc. If sewn directly on a skin garment or moccasins, be aware that holes all the way through the skin makes a weak spot and the skin can tear.

Illustrated are stitches used for applique work. Pull tight.

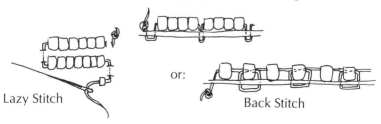

Lazy Stitch

or:

Back Stitch

Half-way Sewn Through: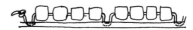

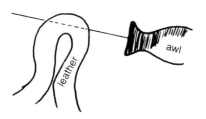

To sew thread or sinew directly onto leather use a sharp needle and an awl.

Pinch the leather and pierce with the awl, then sew through the pre-punched hole with the sharp needle and beads too small for use with a glovers needle.

When doing fashion beadwork, sewing beads directly onto a single layer of material, back the work with non-woven interfacing for strength and durability, especially when filling in areas.

Two Needle Method:

Loopstitch: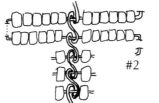

Thread #1 is fastened to the backing only at start and finish.

Three Needle Method:
An unusual style dated 1830-1850.

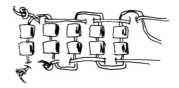

PROJECTS

EARRINGS

SUPPLIES:

Size 11° glass seed beads
3 colors
   (Suggestions to start or use your own combination:
   dark red [wine], light blue, white)
Light blue or white thread
#12 short or sharp needle
Scissors
Beeswax
Glue or clear polish
1 pair ear wires or earring findings

Thread your needle with a workable length of thread (about 12" will be enough to get started if you are unaccustomed to working with these supplies). Pull the thread over the beeswax once to lightly coat the thread.

Tie one red bead on one end of the thread. (Work with the thread as a single strand at all times with the beads.) String 10 red beads and go back through the first (tied bead) and second bead to form a circle.

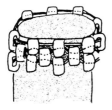

Continue with the gourd stitch in red beads for 4 rows. Follow with 4 rows of light blue, 2 rows of white, 4 rows of light blue, and 4 rows of red. Review the general instructions for the gourd stitch and remember, the pattern should look like tiny bricks laid in a circle pattern. Pull each row tight so that your cylinder of beadwork will be firm.

*   *To add more thread – take the needle off the thread when you have about 4" tail remaining, tie on a new length of waxed thread and knot several times close to the beadwork. Reinforce the knot with glue or clear nail polish and do not trim yet.*

When the last row of red beads are in place, go through that last row one more time with the thread to reinforce the row that will be holding the fringe.

FRINGE:

String 7 red beads, 7 blue, 7 white, 5 red, 3 blue, 1 white, 3 blue, 5 red, 7 white, 7 blue, 7 red, then put your needle back through the same bead the thread came from, IN THE OPPOSITE DIRECTION (see illustration for clarification) making a loop of beaded fringe. Repeat the fringe step for each of the 5 lower beads in the last row of gourd stitch work. If possible, when you have finished the last fringe loop, go through one more bead and then tie the last knot and reinforce with glue or polish.

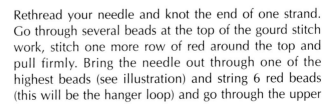

FINISHING THE TOP AND ATTACHING EARWIRE:

Rethread your needle and knot the end of one strand. Go through several beads at the top of the gourd stitch work, stitch one more row of red around the top and pull firmly. Bring the needle out through one of the highest beads (see illustration) and string 6 red beads (this will be the hanger loop) and go through the upper

most bead directly across the circle. Go back through the hanger loop beads and into the same bead the loop originated from and around the top circle one more time to reinforce the hanger loop.

* *If at some bead there is too much thread to let one more strand pass through, stop and tie a knot close to the bead and reinforce with glue or polish.*

Hang from your favorite earring finding. Trim all knot tails when dry and repeat the entire process one more time for your complete pair.

VARIATION:

This same process can also produce a very attractive bolo tie or cord belt. Use a cord of your choice about 32" long for a tie and for a belt a long enough piece to tie comfortably around you. Vary the number of beads to cover the cord and attach the first row to the cord about 1-1/2" from the end. Sewing the beadwork to the cord about every one-half inch, follow the directions to finish and fringe. Add a bolo tie ring or tie it around your waist.

LARGER VARIATION:

To make a key ring, use a wooden dowel about 2-1/2" long as a base and finish with a screw eye and split ring (see illustration).

LOOMED BARRETTES

SUPPLIES:

A pair of 2" metal hair barrettes
2 matching pieces of loom beadwork approx. 2-1/4" x
   1/2 " each
Household cement
Scissors
Sharp needle and thread
Beeswax
Beads for border
Adhesive tape or artist's tape (not masking or
   transparent, they age too quickly and will let go)
Soft pencil (not ballpoint, it permanently stains
   leather)
Thimble

Prepare the loomwork for the barrette.

Tie the warp threads close to the beadwork and turn
the knot fringes under and tape the underside with a
small square of tape.

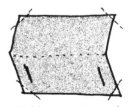

Prepare the leather for the barrette. Fold one piece of
leather in half and mark with pencil the size of the
loomwork. Measure from the folded edge. Trim the
leather to the size of the beadwork and cut the corners
on an angle (see illustration).

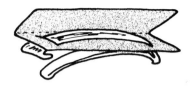

Open the leather and mark the fold. Lay the barrette on the leather and mark approximately 1/8" from each end of the barrette. Cut a slit approximately 3/16" long at each mark centered in one half of the leather (see illustration).

Fit the leather over the barrette, as shown, and glue in place with very small dots of cement. (Too much glue will cause the leather to harden, making further sewing very difficult.)

ATTACHING LOOMWORK TO THE LEATHER:

Prepare a needle and waxed thread, knotting only one of the thread ends.

Place loomwork on top of leather, now attached to the barrette, to make sure the beadwork and the leather are very close to the same size. If not, trim the leather slightly to fit the beadwork. If leather is too small, you will probably have to remove the leather and start again or make a smaller piece of beadwork for your barrette.

Sew a couple of stitches through the leather and beadwork to secure them while putting on the border. Bring the needle out at an edge to begin the border.

THE BORDER

Use the two bead edging stitch. Be sure to catch both layers of leather as well as the outside thread of the beadwork with every stitch. When you turn a corner you will understand why we trimmed the corners at a tiny angle. The border stitch turns an angled corner much smoother than a squared corner.

Reinforce all knots with glue or polish and trim the thread when the knots are dry.

There is a lot of work in a nice barrette, but the beauty and compliments will make it all worthwhile.

QUILL PREPARATION & STORAGE

If you would like to use quills in your beadwork projects here are some suggestions for preparing them for use:

Soak quills overnight in a solution of water and mild detergent, not any stronger than you would wash dishes with and maybe even a little weaker. The next day the quills will be soft and clean, and easily trimmed with scissors.

Cut the sharp ends off the quills and if you are using only a certain size quill, trim to the size you need.

Using a long, sharp, heavy needle, make a hole from end to end through the spongy inner material of the quill and lay it aside to dry. Quills are now ready for use in your project.

Store the quills in a sealed jar or plastic bag with a moth ball to discourage any critters from moving in with your quills.

MINI-ROSETTE EARRINGS

Attach jump ring
for detachable "drop."

SUPPLIES:
Scrap of interfacing
Scrap of suede or lightweight leather or felt
Seed beads (size 10, 11 or 12)
Sharp needle
Thread
Scissors for small detail work
Pencil
Earring post with saucer or clip finding suitable for a
    rosette

Refer to general rosette instructions in this volume and make two identical rosettes about 3/4" in diameter on the scrap of interfacing material.

Carefully trim the excess interfacing away from the beadwork (trim as closely as possible), but be very careful not to snip the beadwork stitches.

Use the trimmed rosette as a pattern to draw the correct size circle on the leather and trim the leather circle to size.

Snip or punch a small hole in the center of the leather circles. Insert the earring post in the hole.

Connect the leather circle and the beaded interfacing (sandwiching the saucer between) with the two bead edging stitch around the rosette.

Circle of leather
with hole punched.

Insert post with saucer.

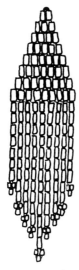

BUGLE BEAD EARRINGS

SUPPLIES:
2° bugle beads
Beading needle
Thread (approx. 1 yard for each earring)
Complimentary color seed beads

1. String 9 bugle beads on the yard of thread. Wrap the tail or knotted end of the thread around the index finger opposite your sewing hand.

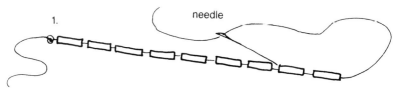

1.

needle

2. Refer to the diagram. Start sewing "backwards" beginning with the second bead from the last one you strung on the thread. Continue sewing backwards until you have lined up all the bugle beads side by side and tie a knot to hold them secure. Leave the long tail thread for now.

2a.

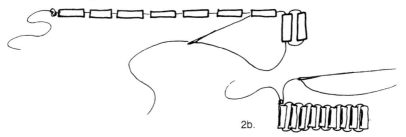

2b.

3. String 2 bugle beads on the thread.

4. Sew between the second and third beads and pull the 2 new bugle beads into a "standing" position.

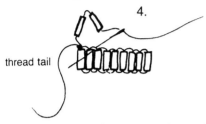

thread tail

5. Sew between beads 1 and 2 and sew up through the first bead of the second row and down the second bead, again through the stitch between 2 and 3 in the first row and up through the second bead in the new row.

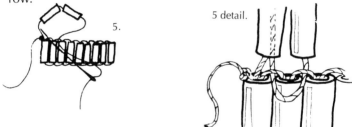

5.

5 detail.

6. Add one bugle bead, sew between the next two beads in the bottom row and up through the new bead.

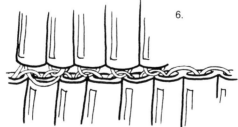

6.

(Drawings are shown loose for clarity; pull your stitches tight.)

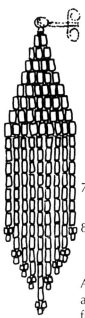

7. Continue adding one bugle bead at a time to the end of the row.

8. Go back to step #3 and diagram #4, and add the next row until you get to the final two bugle beads at the top.

At this point you must decide what "finding" you will attach to your earring and sew it in place between the final two bugle beads. Add a tiny jump ring here to use the bugle bead earring as a detachable "drop" to add to your mini-rosette earring. Just slip the jumping over the post and you have an entirely new earring.

Refer to the fringe section of this volume and choose the style of fringe you like to finish your earrings.

When all fringes are complete, if your last stitch has not brought your needle back to the original starting point (where the knot and thread "tail" are), weave the needle through the stitches back to the "tail" and tie both ends of the thread and reinforce with glue or clear nail polish, trim and hide the knot in one of the bugle beads.

Vary your design with different colors or finish a diamond shape with or without fringe.

Another variation is to use larger bugle or tube beads. Finish the first row as above and the remaining pyramid with larger seed beads and the fringe with a combination of seed beads and large bugles.

Practice often and use your imagination. Your creations will reflect your good taste for many years!

REFERENCES

"Bead a Rosette," *The American Indian Hobbyist,* Vol. 1, No. 3, Nov. 1954, p. 2.

Chandler, M.G. & Kracinski, D.A., 1962, "Unusual Beadwork Techniques" Park I, *American Indian Tradition,* 1962, Vol. 8, No. 5, p. 197-206.

Feder, Norman, 1961. "A Note On: An Unusual Style of Beadwork," *American Indian Tradition,* 1961, Vol. 8, No. 1, p. 41-42.

Gil, Carol A. Bowdoin, 1977. "Native North American Seed Beading Techniques: Park 1 – Woven Items," *Bead Journal,* 1977, Vol. 3, No. 2, p. 42-50.

Gill, Ann E., 1976. *Beadwork* published by Watson-Guptill Publications, New York.

Goodhue, Horace, 1975. *Indian Beadweaving Patterns* published by Bead-craft, St. Paul, Minn.

Herrington, Loren D., 1962. "Charm Bags," *American Indian Tradition,* 1962, Vol. 8, No. 4.

Holsinde, Robert, 1958. *Indian Beadwork* published by Wm. Morrow and Co., Inc., New York.

Hunt, W. Ben, and Burshears, J.F. 'Buck,' 1951. *American Indian Beadwork* published by MacMillan Publishing, New York.

Kracinski, David A., 1963. "Unusual Bead Work Techniques," Park II, *American Indian Tradition,* 1963, Vol. 9, No. 1, p. 38-40.

"Loom Beadwork," *Whispering Wind* published by Louisiana Indian Hobbyist Association, New Orleans, LA. Feb., 1972, p. 68-71.

Orchard, William C., 1929. "Beads and Beadwork of the American Indians," *Heye Foundation Contributions,* Museum of the American Indian, New York, Vol. II, 1929.

Smith, Jerry, March 1968. "Peyote Beadwork," *Indian Craft Series* #1008 published by the California Indian Hobbyist Association, 1968.

Stewart, Ty, 1969. "Peyote Beadwork Technique," *Singing Wire,* Vol. III, No. 1, published by Ty Stewart, Panorama City, CA, Jan. 1969.

Sutton, Scott, January 1969. "Southern Plains Beaded Medallions," *Indian Craft Series* #1018, published by the California Indian Hobbyist Association, 1969.

White, Mary, 1904. *How To Do Beadwork,* re-published by Dover Publications, 1972.

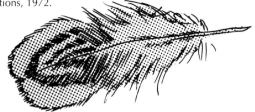

GLOSSARY – INDEX

ABOUT THE AUTHOR...

Z. Susanne Aikman is a graduate of Celina (Ohio) High School, Famous Artists School, The Ohio State University and Metropolitan State College (Denver). Beadwork has been an avocation for more than 25 years. Her professional career includes fine artist, writer, graphic designer, and video and television producer.

Her Eastern Cherokee heritage keeps her close to traditional and spiritual values. Her education and goals bring contemporary concepts to her work which includes: photography, videography, drawing, painting, graphics, sculpture, and writing. Her work is represented in private collections all across the U.S.

pages for your
notes, ideas, &
inspirations

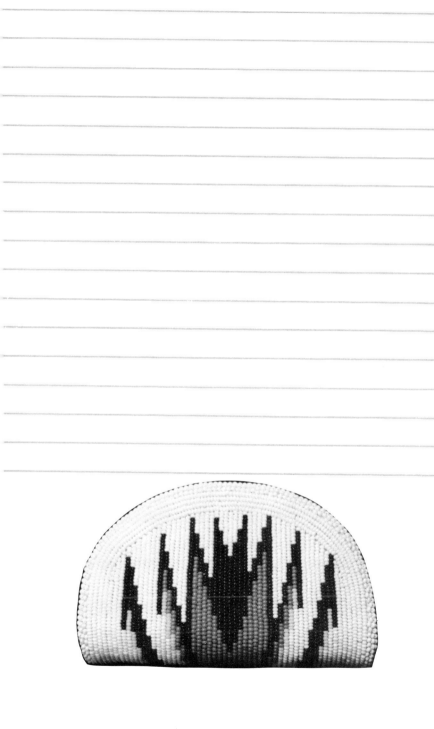